Landmarks.

THE LOST FARM

AND

OTHER POEMS.

BY

JOHN JAMES PIATT,

AUTHOR OF "WESTERN WINDOWS," ETC.

BOSTON:

JAMES R. OSGOOD & COMPANY,

Late Ticknor & Fields, and Fields, Osgood, & Co.

1877.

RIVERSIDE, CAMBRIDGE:
PRINTED BY H. O. HOUGHTON AND COMPANY.

TO

DONN PIATT,

FROM

HIS FRIEND AND KINSMAN.

CONTENTS.

LANDMARKS.

OTHER POEMS.

LANDMARKS.

"GLAD SIGHT, WHEREVER NEW WITH OLD
IS JOIN'D THROUGH SOME DEAR HOME-BORN TIE."

WORDSWORTH.

THE LOST FARM.

THE SCHOOLMASTER'S STORY.

WHEN my strong fathers came into the West,
They chose a tract of land they thought the best:
Near a swift river, in whose constant flow
Peacefully earth and heaven were one below;
Gigantic wardens, on the horizon, stood
Far-circling hills, rough to their tops with wood.

They came, a long and dangerous journey then,
Through paths that had not known of civil men;
With wives and children looking back, and still
Returning long in dreams confusing will,

They came, and in the panther-startled shade
The deep foundations of a State were laid.
The axe, in stalwart hands, with steadfast stroke,
The savage echoes of the forest woke,
And, one by one, breaking the centuries' spell,
The hardy trees, long-crashing, with thunder fell.
The log-house rose, within the solitude,
And civilized the tenants of the wood.
It was not long before the shadow'd mold
Open'd to take the sunshine's gift of gold;
In the dark furrow dropp'd the trusted seed,
And the first harvest bless'd the sower's need.

Oh, dear the memory of their simpler wealth,
Whose hardship nursed the iron flower of health;
Oh, sweet the record of the lives they spent,
Whose breath was peace, whose benison content;
Unenvied now by us, their delicate sons,

The dangers which they braved, those heartier ones!
The Indian's midnight coming, long ago,
And the wolf's howl in nights that shone with snow,
These are but dreams to us (who would but dream),
Pictured far off, heard as lost sounds that seem:
They knew the terror, seventy years gone by,
Of the realities we may not try,
Who left the farm on which my new-born eyes
Saw the great miracle of earth and skies.

The fields were clear'd; the farm-house, girt around
With meadow-lands and orchards, held its ground;
The goodly place had wavering uplands, sweet
With cattle-pastures, hot with ripening wheat.
The house look'd Westward, where the river lay
Shimmering o'er level lands at close of day,
Or, many-twinkling through the autumnal morn,
In the hazy heat rustled the languid corn.

Not far were neighbors—heirs of acres wide,
Or the small farms in which the old divide.
By the close pike, a half-mile off to the north,
The tavern, with old-fashion'd sign thrust forth,
Show'd Washington, a little faded then,
(Too faded now, among new-famous men!)
And, close beside, the blacksmith-shop was found,
In August noons obtrusive with its sound,
Or late in winter eves, a welcome sight,
Burning and brightening through with bursting
light!

Such was the farm—how dear to my regret!—
Whose fresh life runs into my bosom yet.
My dreams may bear me thither even now.
Again, with eager heart and sunburnt brow,
Homesick at times, I take a noiseless train,
Wandering, breath-like, to my home again;

See my glad brothers, in the June-sweet air,
Toss the green hay, the hot sheaves of harvest bear;
The fireside warms into my heart—how plain!
And my lost mother takes her boy again;
My sisters steal around me tenderly—
And all that can not be yet seems to be!

In thirty years what changes there have been!—
How disappear the landmarks that were seen!
If I should go to seek my boyhood's place,
What chart would show the way, what guide would
trace?

New people came. Around the tavern grew
New dwellings and new manners—all things new.
The impetus of something in the land
(Some gold, unseen, diviners understand),
Some mystic loadstone of the earth or air,

Drew all the nimble spirits of action there.
The village, not without a conscious pride,
Grew fast and gather'd in the country-side,
Then took the name of town. And now, behold,
A wild, strange rumor through the country roll'd !—
A railroad was projected, East and West,
Which would not slight us, so the shrewd ones guess'd.
Strange men with chain and compass came at last
Among the hills, across the valley pass'd ;
Through field and woodland, pasture, orchard, they
Turn'd not aside, but kept straight on their way.
Old farmers threaten'd, but it did no good—
The quick conservatives of the neighborhood.
"We do not want it!" many said, and one,
"Through field of mine I swear it shall not run!"
And paced his boundary-line with loaded gun.
Others replied (wise, weather-sighted, they!)

"You'll think a little differently, some day.
The wheels of progress will you block—good speed!
(Cut off your nose to spite your face, indeed!)
'T will make the land worth double, where you walk."
"Stuff! stuff!" the old fogies answer'd—"how you
talk!"

The road was open'd. Soon another, down
Northward and Southward, cut across the town:
Both pass'd through meadows where my boyhood
stray'd:
One through the barn within whose mow I play'd.
And then a newer force of circumstance
Took hold and pull'd the place in quick advance:
The lovely river—swift, and deep, and strong—
Upon whose shore I fish'd and idled long,
(The still companion of my dreaming hour,)
Had great advantages of water-power.

Saw-mills and grist-mills, factories builded there,
Cover'd the banks and jarr'd the quiet air.
The river could not sleep nor dream its old
Beautiful dream, in morn or evening gold,
Or as a fallen soul had fitful glance
At its divine and lost inheritance.

The town became a city—growing still,
And growing ever, with a giant's will
Gathering and grasping, changing all it took.
A city sewer was my school-boy brook.
The farm remain'd, but only in the name;
The old associations lived the same.
The approaching city drew its arm around,
And threaten'd more and more the invaded ground;
Near and more near its noises humm'd and groan'd,
(Higher and higher priced the land we own'd!)
My father held his ground, and would not sell.

The stiff wiseacres praised his wisdom well.

At last I came from home. At college long
Absent, at home something, meanwhile, went wrong.
I need not tell the fact. What house is proof,
With jealous threshold and protected roof
Against the subtle foes that every-where
Stand waiting to attack in safest air—
The insidious foes of Fortune or of Fate,
Who plan our ruin while we estimate
Our sum of new success? My father died—
(My mother soon was buried by his side;)
The farm pass'd into speculative hands,
Who turn'd to sudden profit all its lands.
The greedy city seized upon them fast,
And the dear home was swept into the Past.
Across its quiet meadows streets were laid,
White-hot, the dusty thoroughfares of trade.

Where the gray farm-house had its sacred hearth
Sprang buildings hiding heaven and crowding earth.

A score of years were pass'd. Return'd by chance
(A railway accident the circumstance)
To that strange city only known by name,
Unwilling visitor by night I came;
And, sleeping there within some great hotel,
There rose a dream that fills my heart to tell.
I came, a boy—it seem'd not long away—
Close to my father's house at shut of day.
I cross'd the pasture and the orchard where
Glimmer'd the cider-mill in golden air;
The faint, soft tremor of the wandering bell
Of cattle mingled with the old clover-smell.
I leap'd the brook that twinkled darkly bright,
And saw the farm-house dusk'd in mellow light.
The river, painted with the Western gleam,

Show'd through the leaves a Paradisal dream.
By the side-door my father met me then,
My mother kiss'd me in the porch again——
A moment all that was not was! I 'woke
And through my window saw the morning smoke
Of the loud city. And my dream, behold,
Was on the spot of the dear hearth of old!
A man's vain tears hung vague within my eyes.

The Lost Farm underneath the city lies.

THE FORGOTTEN WELL.

BY the old high road I find,
(The weeds their story tell,)
With fallen curb and fill'd with stones,
A long-forgotten well.

The chimney, crumbling near,
A mute historian stands,
Of human joy and human woe—
Far, faded fireside bands!

Here still the apple blows
Its bloom of rose-lit snow;
The rose-tree bless'd some gentle hands
With roses, long ago.

I can not choose but dream
  Of all thy good foredone;
Old alms-giver, thy gifts once more
  Show diamonds in the sun!

From yonder vanish'd home,
  Blithe children therein born;
The mother with her crowing babe;
  The grandsire palsy-worn;

Strong men, whose weighted limbs
  Falter through dust and heat;
Lithe youths in dreamland sowing deeds;
  Shy maidens blushing sweet;

The reaper from his sheaves;
  The mower from his hay—

These take thy freshness in their hearts,
  And pass—my dream—away!

Forgotten by the throng,
  Uncared for and unknown,
None seek thee through the wood of weeds
  Neglect has slowly sown.

Yet, under all, thou'rt there—
  Exhaustless, pure, and cold—
If but the sunshine came to see;
  The fountain ne'er grows old!

TWO HARVESTS.

A MOUND IN THE PRAIRIES.

ALL day the reapers through the wheat
Have wrought amid the sultry heat,
Reaping the harvest wide and fleet.

All day the binders' stooping train
Have swelter'd through the sweating grain,
Binding the bearded sheaves amain :

With shouted jest, with breaks of song,
Lightening their heavy toil along,
A merry-hearted, boisterous throng!

But now, where all alone I stand,
The shocks like tents of gold expand,
The camp of Plenty in the Land!

Through the wide solitude around
Shrills but the empty dream of sound;
The Hours in golden sheaf lie bound.

Bathed in the crimsoning hush of air,
Yon mound, against the twilight bare
Breathes from a deeper twilight there.

The long grass rustled, year by year;
The herded bison thunder'd near;
Bounding in sunshine flew the deer.

The summers went, the summers came—
Years, years, years, years!—and all the same;
November's winding-sheet was flame!

The trees that hedge the prairies in
Have whispers dim of what has been,
Traditions of their crumbled kin.

Yon mound was still while centuries fled
And at their feet forgot their dead;
Nothing was ask'd and nothing said.

Now, vast with twilight's glamoury,
It whispers weirdly unto me;
Great dusky mirages I see.

In far-off days the Atlantic morn
Came not to find a world new-born;
Wide fields of sunshine shake with corn.

Lo, here an elder harvest land,
With many another reaper band!—
The tents of Plenty thickly stand.

All day the binders' stooping train,
Sweltering through the sweating grain,
Bind the hot-bearded sheaves amain:

With shouted jest, with breaks of song,
Lightening their heavy toil along,
A merry-hearted, boisterous throng!

And, as in those fair fields we see,
Through Bible-gates of memory,
In the high East shine beauteously:

Some Boaz owns the harvest plain,
Where, following the reapers' train,
See, Ruth, the gleaner, walks again!

Love, that had flush'd the centuries,
Lovely, as yonder, dwells with these;
And Faith, with nations at her knees!

The same sun shines, the same earth glows,
With the same transient joys and woes
The last man as the first man knows.

For Nature, swarthy mother, warms
(However changed their faces, forms,)
One human family in her arms!

The cattle low from field to fold;
The harvesters in evening gold
Leave the dusk shocks—the tale is told!

The silence falls, the twilight deep;
Myriads of morns the grasses creep
Across vast solitudes of sleep.

The herded bison thunder'd near;
Bounding in sunshine flew the deer;
The long grass rustled year by year.

Wolf, deer, and bison!—lo! the Wind,
A huntsman wild, to mad and blind,
Flinging his fiery torch behind!

MOORE'S CHIMNEY.

I.

THE SHADOW-LAND.

ROUND us lies a Land of Shadow, not a footstep echoes o'er;
Song of peace and cry of battle falter, dying, evermore.

War-fires in the vales are leaping, with the glaring dance of war,
But the fiercely-gleaming faces are a painted dream afar.

O'er the valley, clothed in shadow, sunlit stands the startled deer,

From the cliff against the morning flashing away,
breath-like, with fear.

Lo, the golden light of morning o'er the Land of
Shadow cast,
Where the tomahawk is buried in the grave-mound
of the Past!

Nothing of that Land remains, now, save these gray
historic trees,
Shaking through their glittering branches dews of
olden memories!

II.

THE RUIN.

Here among the greenery hidden, warder of that
Shadow-Land,
Near the noisy-trampled highway, see the old dead
chimney stand!—

Hidden from the busy highway 'mong the cherries
large and low,
Whose new blossoms fill the breezes with a gentle
drift of snow!

Dead!—no more a flame is leaping through it toward
the wintry cold;
Dead!—no more its smoke is wreathing woodlands
deep and dim and old.

Dead!—no more its azure welcome gladdens eyes
that houseless roam;
Dead!—no more it seems uplifting incense from the
heart of Home!

Gone the hands that shook the forest, burying in the
furrow'd soil
Careful seeds of trust returning harvest-guerdon for
their toil.

Gone the hearts that made pale faces, when the
wolves came starved with cold,
And the fireside still was waiting through the twi-
light snows of old.

Gone the homely cabin-threshold, with the feet that
cross'd it o'er;
Gone the closely-gather'd household, with their dwell-
ing low and poor.

Yet I see a light of sparkles redden up old evenings
wild,
Like the fancies sent to wander up the chimney by
a child.

Hearts, I think, there may be, somewhere, echoing
through the vanish'd door,
Dreaming dreams returning, hearing footsteps from
the crumbled floor.

Children, whose new lives were darken'd here with
shades of sudden fears,
May be children, wandering hither, while old gray
men lose their years;

They may hear the red-man's voices through the
night the silence start,
And, awaking, the old terror shiver newly through
the heart.

You may find them growing weary, faltering through
the busy lands,
Wrinkled by the years their faces, shaken by the
years their hands.

Of them here no token lingers, save the chimney
gray and low,
With a gleam of lighted faces from a fireside long
ago!

WALKING TO THE STATION.

I WANDER down the woodland lane,
  That to the turnpike greenly steals:
In breathless twilight-gold, again,
  To wait the far-approaching wheels;
To hear the driver's horn once more
  Wind all around the river wood,
Shy echoes start along the shore
  And thrill the bosky solitude.

Here, coming back last night, I 've found,
  Of folk familiar once, how few!—
Some, blacken'd names in graveyard ground,
  Forgotten on the farms they knew.

In our quick West the ruthless plow
  Spares not dear landmarks to displace;
The old Home, so long regretted, now
  Stared at me with a stranger's face!

Hark! the vague hum of wheels is blown,
  Fitful, across the evening calm——
No; 't is the far-off sound, well known
  To boyish ears, of Mower's dam.
I started later than I ought,
  It may be, and the stage is pass'd——
Fond fancy!—disenchanting thought,
  That will not let the fancy last!

Ah, broken dream! The wheels no more
  Ring faint beyond the Southern hill;
No longer down the valley roar,
  Waking the twilight bridges still;

No more the lonely farm it cheers
  To see the tavern's added light——
The stage is gone these seventeen years ;
  I walk to meet the train to-night.

Yet here 's the crossing (ne'er a trace
  Of the old toll-gate toward the mill)—
The parting and the meeting place,
  Dear, dear to homesick memory still !
Oh, schoolboy-time of joy and woe,
  Of sad farewells, of blithe returns !—
I feel again the pang to go,
  The homeward rapture in me burns !

A sound grows busy with the breeze,
  A nearing roar, a glancing light,
A tremor through yon darkling trees—
  The fiery pant, the rushing might !

The head-light glares, the whistle screams;
  I cross the field, the platform gain.
Give back, for old regrets and dreams,
  To-morrow, love and dear ones, train!

GRANDFATHER WRIGHT.

HE knew of the great pioneering days,
And the dread Indian times that only live
In dreams of old men when the ember-ghost
Of long December evenings, Memory,
Rising from the white ashes of the hearth
And from the ashes of their outburnt lives,
Haunts them, and fills them with a tender breath
From the rough forests, full of wolves and deer,
Where their young hearts made the fierce land their own.

FARTHER.

FAR-OFF a young State rises, full of might:
I paint its brave escutcheon. Near at hand
See the log cabin in the rough clearing stand;
A woman by its door, with steadfast sight,
Trustful, looks Westward, where, uplifted bright,
Some city's Apparition, weird and grand,
In dazzling quiet fronts the lonely land,
With vast and marvelous structures wrought of light,
Motionless on the burning cloud afar:—
The haunting vision of a time to be,
After the heroic age is ended here,
Built on the boundless, still horizon's bar
By the low sun, his gorgeous prophecy
Lighting the doorway of the pioneer!

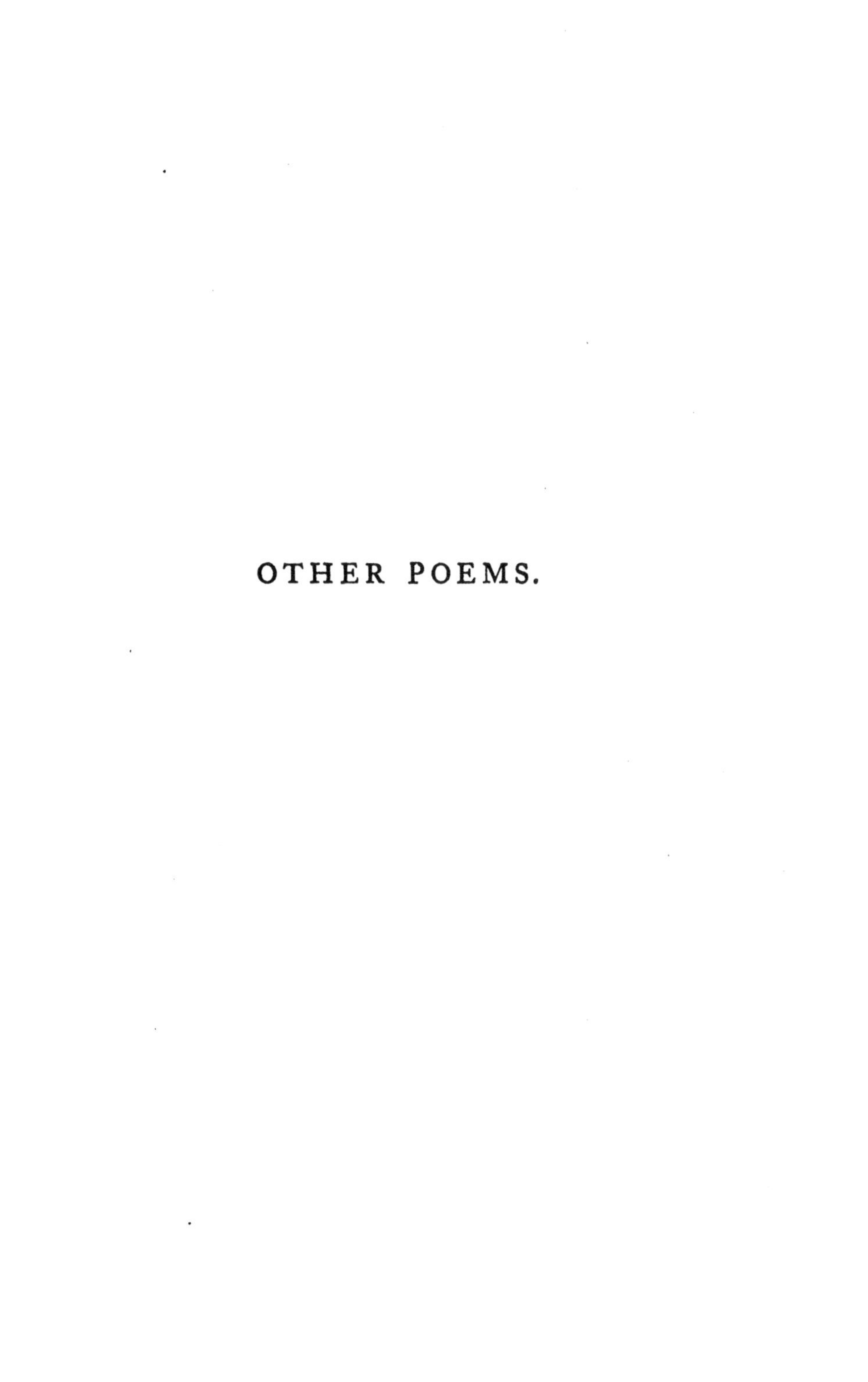

OTHER POEMS.

THE THREE WORK-DAYS.

SO much to do, so little done!
In sleepless eyes I saw the sun;
His beamless disk in darkness lay,
The dreadful ghost of YESTERDAY!

So little done, so much to do!
The morning shone on harvests new;
In eager light I wrought my way,
And breathed the spirit of TO-DAY!

So much to do, so little done!
The toil is past, the rest begun;
Though little done, and much to do,
TO-MORROW Earth and Heaven are new!

THE LOST GENIUS.

A GIANT came to me when I was young,
My instant will to ask—
My earthly Servant, from the earth he sprung
Eager for any task!

"What wilt thou, O my Master?" he began;
"Whatever can be," I.
"Say thy first wish—whate'er thou wilt I can,"
The Strong Slave made reply.

"Enter the earth and bring its riches forth,
For pearls explore the sea."
He brought, from East and West and South and North,
All treasures back to me!

"Build me a palace wherein I may dwell."
"Awake and see it done,"
Spake his great voice at dawn. Oh, miracle!
That glitter'd in the sun!

"Find me the princess fit for my embrace,
The vision of my breast;
For her search every clime and every race."
My yearning arms were bless'd!

"Get me all knowledge." Sages with their lore,
And poets with their songs,
Crowded my palace halls at every door,
In still, obedient throngs!

"Now bring me wisdom." Long ago he went;
(The cold task harder seems:)

He did not hasten with the last content—
    The rest, meanwhile, were dreams!

Houseless and poor, on many a trackless road,
    Without a guide, I found
A white-hair'd phantom, with the world his load
    Bending him to the ground!

"I bring thee wisdom, Master." Is it he,
    I marvel'd then, in sooth?
"Thy palace-builder, beauty-seeker, see!"
    I saw the Ghost of Youth!

CONFLAGRATION.

I.

PLAYING with little children on the hearth,
An hour ago—
With fitful mirth
Their gentle eyes were lighted—lo! the Flame,
Like a lithe Fairy, to their fancies came,
Whispering whispers low!

II.

All sleep. The harmless Fairy wakes and chases
Across the floor, and from the darkness crawls,
Clambering up the walls,
And looks into the children's sleeping faces;
Now through the window shines
On the dew-burden'd vines;

Then, Fiend-like, leaps,
Aloof,
Upon the roof!
The city sleeps.
It waves its myriad hands,
And laughs and dances, a maniac lost from bands!

III.

The scared bells ring!—
All sleepers, wakening, start
With fluttering heart!
Look! the gigantic Thing
The unimprison'd Fury, tosses high
Bloodiest arms against the frighten'd sky,
O'er streets that glare with men! Midnight gives way
To the flame-cradled day!
White Fear and red Confusion mingle cries:
"Arise! arise!

The city is in flame!"
The hearth-born Terror keeps its hurrying march,
The world aghast before, the clouds its victory-arch,
(The Larés on their altars die,
The wives and children fly :)
And ashes are its fame!

THE NEW HOUSE.

I.

THE BUILDING.

A STRANGER in the village street,
Shines the new house in morning light—
No quick enchantment sprung by night,
A vision for the sun, complete,
Like that the Arabian story shows:
For the slow toil of hours and days,
With steadfast hands and stalwart blows,
Wrought with the builder's brain, to raise
This temple, yet unconsecrate,
Of Home and Household Deities,
The stronghold of Domestic Peace,
Familiar Church and private State!

The builder he has watch'd it long,
Since first the pencil-plan was made
And the deep under-stone was laid,
The fast foundation firm and strong,
Through slow processes, day by day,
While floors were fix'd and rafters hung,
Till now—the workmen pass'd away—
He wakes from slumber, blithe and young:
Behold, at last, his work is done!—
His house-in-air no longer dream,
Illumined by the morning gleam,
Transfigured by the rising sun!

II.

THE DWELLERS.

Come at Morning—you shall see
What a blissful company
Enter in the open door!

Children, children, evermore,
Dancing, singing, laughing, play,
Making merry holiday—
Happy faces, garments gay !—
Introducing Fairy-land,
Back to barren desert sand
Bringing flowers flown from earth :
The long coming-in of Birth!

Come at Midnight—you shall see
What a ghostly company
Pass from out the open door!
Old men, old men, evermore,
Wrinkled, dusty, travel-spent,
Burden-bearers bow'd and bent,
Songless, sighing, halting, slow,
In funereal garments go,
But, upon the threshold, lo!

Sudden children, vanish there,
Lost in light and lifting air,
Beautiful with blissful breath:
The long going-forth of Death!

THE PEACH-BLOSSOMS.

SENT TO ME IN THE CITY, WITH THE WORDS,

"IT IS SPRING."

IT was a gentle gift to send,
This thought in blossoms from a friend:
Within my city room
I seem to breathe the country air,
While April's kisses every-where
Start Earth's brown cheeks to bloom!

Oh, beautiful the welcome sight!
(Flushing my paper as I write,
My words seem blossoming!)—

The lovely lighted snow that falls
Rosy around the cottage walls,
A miracle of Spring!

Dream-like, I hear the sunny hum
Of swarming bees ; low voices come
Familiar, close, and dear:
I hardly know if I am there,
Or, shutting out the noisy air,
Those birds are singing here!

To the dry city's restless heart
What tender influence ye impart,
My blossoms, soft and wild!
Ah! from this barren cell I feel
Your subtle wand, enchanting, steal
Me to the Past—a child!

A child whose laughter-lighted face
Breaks from some happy door, a-chase
For new-wing'd butterflies:
The wind, how merrily, takes his hair!—
Sing, birds, and keep him ever there
With world-forgetting eyes!

Most gracious miracle of Spring
That gives the dead tree, blossoming,
Its resurrection hour!
Lo! Memory lifts her wizard bough,
(That seem'd as bare and barren,) now
Within my soul, in flower!

THE YELLOW LEAF:

IN THE POET'S BOOK.

"WHISPER, Yellow Leaf, to me
Thy forgotten history."

"One far spring-time, green and young,
On a sunny bough we hung.

"Happiest of green leaves were we,
Fluttering glad on the green tree.

"Merrily fairy moonbeams play'd,
Dancing through our dancing shade.

"Deck'd with Morn's lost jewelry,
Full of singing birds were we.

"Through the May and through the June
We danced every breeze's tune.

"Ask not where my kin are flown;
I am old and here alone.

"Their far summer-time was brief;
I am here a Yellow Leaf.

"Sunbeams grew cold and winds grew wild—
Kiss the Summer's orphan child!"

"Whisper, Yellow Leaf, to me
Why the poet treasures thee."

"That far Spring, when we were young,
In our shade a maiden sung;

"And his life a blossoming tree,
Danced with leaves as glad as we.

"But those blissful leaves at last
Flutter'd, falling, to the Past.

"See his song along with me,
Yellow Leaf of Memory!

"Book-marks of his life we lie,
Brother-leaves, the song and I.

"Song and leaf, from that far Spring
Dreams of joy and woe we bring.

"Let the song again be sung:
I again am green and young.

"And a maiden sings below:
Sun-leaf'd shadows wreathe her brow.

"Summer-time and love were brief:
Love the Poet's Yellow Leaf!"

THE UNBIDDEN GUEST.

ON THE DEATH OF A BRIDE.

AH, many doors He jars with welcome knock!
To the o'erburthen'd breast,
Through the dark hall, His footstep gives no shock,
But seems a sound of rest.

O Uninvited! every street hath such—
Enough, enough for Thee!
Hunger and Cold, they bless thy kindred touch
And ask thy company!

Lo, one glad house by love had lighted been
With his first, soft, sweet Moon,

And Life, the bidden guest, had just come in—
  Follow'd by Death how soon!

Sudden the lamps grow dark, a stealthy cold
  Palsies the joyous room;
The young man's place is taken by the old,
  Dark, deaf, dumb, sightless Groom!

The marriage greetings falter in speechless pain!
  Blithe bells—your toll we hear!
The bridal party goes—the funeral train;
  The bridal-bed's the bier!

APPLE-GATHERING.

THE beautiful apples, so golden and mellow,
They will fall at a kiss of the breeze,
While it breathes through the foliage frosty and yellow
And the sunshine is filling the trees!
Though high in the light wind they gladly would linger
On the boughs where their blossoms were found,
Yet they drop at a breath, at the touch of a finger
They shatter their cores on the ground!

Through the morn of October while Autumn is trying
With all things to make-believe Spring,

How the leaves of the orchard around us are flying!—
  The heavens with jubilee ring!
The ladders in breezes of sunshine are swinging,
  The farmer-boys gladden and climb:
To gather the fruit they are swaying and singing—
  Glad hearts to glad voices keep time!

Far down the bright air they are happy to listen
  To the noise of the mill and the flail,
And the waters that laugh as they leap and they glisten
  From the dam that is lighting the vale!
The wild flutter of bells that so dreamily rises
  From glades where the cows wander slow,
And the laughter of faces in childish surprises
  When the wind flings an apple below!

Oh, see! in the trees that are drinking the splendor,
How the gladness of boyhood is seen!—
How they shake all the branches so windy and slender,
And a quick golden rain is between!
High and higher they climb, till the grasses are cover'd
With the fruits that were sweet April flowers,
And the yellowing leaves that all over them hover'd
Flutter down with the apples in showers!

The harvests are garner'd, the meadows are burning,
At sunset, in golden and brown;
The apples are gather'd, the wagons returning:
The Winter may bluster and frown!
The blind-drifting snows may make barren the even,
Dark twilights may shiver with rain;
But the apples and cider by Summer are given—
Give Winter to Summer again!

CÆSAR SALUTED.

[JULY, 1870.]

Cæsar, morituri te salutant."

[From the German of Albert Traeger.]

IS it enough, now? Nations into strife
  To goad, your cloudy soul has ponder'd long;
The Slaughterers you have bidden whet the knife.
  The Cæsar nods, and rages his wild throng.
But while they nod to you with their hot cries,
  The Dying, to the arena who move fast,
Look you, and see the pallid Ghosts arise,
  That stern and solemn gather, hurrying past!
  Do you not know them—feel no sting at last?—
    "Cæsar, the Dead salute you."

Where gay-cheek'd Vice her pleasure-house has set
  For over-feasts of Horror, there erewhile
Shatter'd they lay upon the pavement, yet
  Keeping the oath you swore to with a smile:
First victims to the death-tools, ever more
  Your wit has tried to perfect: there lay still
In bloody blouse and the red cap, you wore
  Yourself to court the Republic in until
  The Butcher, silent, on them crept to kill—
    "Cæsar, the Dead salute you."

Those, too, who did not win the bright, quick death
  Of heroes, sword in hand and smile on face—
In Cayenne's fever-swamps who spent their breath,
  With that dry guillotine dying apace;
Those who in prisons linger'd till the chain
  Dropp'd but with life away; those who, outworn

With sharp, home-longing, ever-gnawing pain,
  Saw their last light in exile-lands, forlorn;
  Hair-blanch'd with grief, those left at home to mourn—
      "Cæsar, the Dead salute you."

And, see, these come with open wounds, who chose
  After your eagles' flights to follow, these
Whose days found in your battles early close—
  To whom you said: "The Empire, it is Peace;"
For Liberty, you promised, to each fight
  You led them: when their blood gave victory,
With scornful smile, after your triumph-light,
  You dug another grave for Liberty,
  So that the earth a graveyard seem'd to be—
      "Cæsar, the Dead salute you."

From the Black Sea they rise and gather round;
  Out of the Italian plains the Sleepers wake,
Who, freed by you, then saw their native ground
  The after-burden of your armies take;
And those sent far across the Atlantic tide
  To meet in Mexico their fatal blight,
There where a second time your sword was tried
  At the Republic with malignant spite,
  And where your star first lost its early light—
    "Cæsar, the Dead salute you."

From out his Tomb is risen another wraith—
  (Rest in the Invalides he finds no more:)
The German war-cry, "Victory or Death!"
  Has proved his sign of ruin once before;
In his gray cloak and the little hat he stands
  Ready for march, the Ancestor of your reign,

But no war-fire his hollow eye commands:
Backward his finger points to *St. Helene,*
As if he sigh'd that still grave to regain—
"Cæsar, the Dead salute you."

IF.

STRONG little Monosyllable between
Desire and joy, between the hand and heart
Of all our longing; dreary death's-head seen
Ere our quick lips to touch the nectar part!
O giant dwarf, making the whole world cling
To thy cold arm before the infant feet
Of frail resolves can walk, man-like, complete,
Steep mountain-roads of high accomplishing!
Dim dragon in the way of our designing,
No Red-Cross Knight may vanquish! Though most brave,
Strong Will before thee crouches, a mute slave—
Faith dies to feel thee in her path declining!
If! thou dost seem to our poor human sense
The broken crutch of our blind providence!

THE CHRYSALIS.

LOOK! a chrysalis, dry and old,
Coffin of a worm, I hold:
'T is no lovely thing you see—
All of beauty yet must be;
You must wait a while, till Spring,
For the blossom, for the wing.
Call it by whatever name,
Couch or coffin, 't is the same.
Deeper down than Science sees
In old wells of mysteries,
(With her mirror'd face below,
Like a wondering child's a-glow,)
Farther far than sagest seeks,
Far as stars that shine in creeks,

Lo! in this unlovely shell
Maskéd Miracle doth dwell,
Old as Heaven, young as Earth!
God breathes and all death is birth:
At his breath and touch, in Spring,
Flutter, flower!—blossom, wing!

LONG AGO.

THOUGH for the soul a lovely Heaven awaits,
Through years of woe,
The Paradise with angels in its gates
Is Long Ago.

The heart's lost Home! Ah, thither winging ever
In silence, show
Vanishing faces!—but they vanish never
In Long Ago!

Ye toil'd through desert sands to reach To-morrow,
With footsteps slow,
Poor Yesterdays!—Immortal gleams ye borrow
In Long Ago.

The world is dark: backward our thoughts are
    yearning,
  Our eyes o'erflow:
Sweet Memories, angels to our tears returning,
  Leave Long Ago.

We climb: child-roses to our knees are climbing,
  From valleys low;
To call us back, dear birds and brooks are rhyming
  In Long Ago.

Hands clasp'd, tears shed, sad songs are sung!—
    the fair,
  Beloved ones, lo!
Shine yonder, through the angel-gates of air,
  In Long Ago!

THE NEW COMING.

SHE comes again! She comes again! On the
new earth once more!
The children sweet, they meet and greet and pull
her to the door!

Blithe maiden, dancing home her song! Oh, echoes
sad, depart!
Her smile 's the key in every door of the prison of
the heart!

All things remember, seeing her—her traveling choir
the birds!
What singing in the sunshine, and what lowing of
the herds!

The lambs, that only Winter knew, have like a gar-
land bound her—
As if they knew her long ago, all gladdening dance
around her!

The trees she only looks upon—green leaves begin
to grow!
The orchard blushes! Is it snow?—but oh! how
fragrant snow!

All things are in the sunny air, whate'er can learn
to fly;
The very worm has brighest wings—in its heaven,
the butterfly!

The Spring! The Spring! She is here again—her
train the gentlest hours!
And the last of the snow, she is smiling so, forgets
it was not—flowers!

CONFIDENCES:

IN A BOOK OF LIKES AND DISLIKES.*

1. MY favorite virtue, what is that? Ah me,
I'll "make a virtue of Necessity!"

2. That ancient apple-eater I like, madam—
The frontispiece of all history—the Old Adam.

3. Tyrants and traitors, bloody-handed men—
I think of these with hesitating pen,
And lo! from graves abhorr'd and flowerless rise

* Written after the following printed indications: 1. Write your favorite virtue. 2. Favorite character in history. 3. The character in history you despise most. 4. Favorite prose author. 5. Favorite poet. 6. Favorite occupation. 7. Favorite color. 8. Favorite flower. 9. Favorite food. 10. Favorite name. 11. Favorite motto. 12. What you dislike most. 13. What you consider the greatest happiness on earth. 14. Your pet name. 15. Full signature.

(But Nero's once had flowers) their ghosts and
cries!—
They claim appeal with pale, imploring look:
"The Supreme Court—the True Historian's
Book!"

4. My pet of authors, must I name, in prose?
I'm sure I know not. The dear Lord only knows!

5. The children of the Muse, nor great nor small,
I can but see the Mother's face in all
Reflected. Some have names, as—thus and thus.
Before and after walks Anonymous.

6. With "good intentions," wavering to and fro,
To pave those scorching sidewalks Down Below!

7. The ebon Black that makes the star more bright,
The White wherein all colors end in light.

8. Rose, Lily, and Violet—the lovely Three
That represent their race in poetry.

9. " Sour grapes."

10. I think that name, of all the host,
I like the best is——hers I love the most!

11. "*Sic transit gloria Mundi.*" (Let it pass!)

12. To see my death's-head's vanity in a glass.

13. The earliest Dream of Happiness, at most
To dream—nor wake to see its latest ghost.

14. 'T is closed on Memory's lips, how dear!

15. Now, that
I 've answer'd, I remain, J. J. P.

CARPE DIEM.

TO-DAY I can not choose but share
The indolence of earth and air;
In dreamful languor lying,
I see, like thistle-flowers that sail
Adown some hazed autumnal vale,
The Hours to Lethé flying.

The hour-glass twinkles in the sun;
Unchanged its ceaseless course is run
Through ever-changeful weathers—
"*Time flies*," its motto: 't is no crime,
I think, to pluck the wings of Time,
And sleep upon his feathers!

SUNSHINE IN RAIN.

THE rain darkles down over woodland and town,
The clouds are all hid in the gray of the rain ;
The wind creeps out of the mist in the meadow,
And beats the wet rose at the pane.

On the honeysuckle porch in the shadow
The little child lightens the darken'd floor;
He claps at the storm with his happy hands,
He laughs at the thunder's roar!

Ah, why is he glad while the meadows are sad,
And our voices are lower'd in graver replies?
But so many rainbows spring up o'er the storm
From his heart to his merry eyes!

BREVIA.

SUCCESS.

THE noblest goal is never reach'd, because
    Ever withdrawn by the high god that draws;
And he who says, content, "Success is mine,"
Gaining the world, has lost the soul divine.

KEEPING A ROSE'S COMPANY.—A PERSIAN FABLE.

A TRAVELER, toiling on a weary way,
Found in his path a piece of fragrant clay.
"This seems but common earth," says he, "but how
Delightful!—it is full of sweetness now!
Whence is thy fragrance?" From the clay there grows
A voice: "I have been very near a rose."

FOR ———.

IF poor the words I breathe you,
  Oh, magic be their power!—
What lovely wreaths shall wreathe you
  If wishes come to flower!

POPULARITY AND FAME.

I.

POST-HASTE one flies—at noisy inns she gossips on
    the way,
Where staring boys applaud and shout, and men in
    liveries gay:
Her business is in yonder town, her journey lasts
    to-day.

II.

One travels slow—at first her inns are houses for the
    poor;

Then mayors wait at city gate and kings at palace
door:
To the world's end she journeys on, her road is ev-
ermore.

WINTER SUNSET.

THE winter day is done:
From early morn blown over restless crowds
Of slow-advancing clouds,
With chilly, azure-lighted intervals,
Now—large and low, beneath their lifted vail—
Breathlessly bright! the sun
Against the eastern distance falls,
Reddening the far forests, empty and cold,
Whence the dumb river draws its icy trail
Through valley-farms the barren hills enfold,
And on the slope, under the spark-like spire,
The village windows shiver, all afire!

FOR SCULPTURE.

Lo, Sleep binds over the weary angel Life,
Whose globe, his care, turns idly from his hand,
With all its continents of toil and strife,
With all its tossing seas and shifting sand!

A LOST KINGDOM OF GODS.

The vast Olympian Heaven vanishes
Like the frail wreck of clouds that travel slow
After a thunder-storm, when eastward far
They sink, forever fainter, lower, down
In evening dusk among dark mountain peaks,
With vague unpurposed thunders, nerveless bolts
Of dull forgetful lightnings; and its King,
Who made an earthquake if he bent his brows,

Moves with his kind in half-forgotten dreams,
Such as we dream, and, waking, find are naught,
But feel their nothing present in all the air.

TASKING THE MUSE.

Thy housekeeper the goddess will not be—
  Make task-work for the Muse and she will fly;
Her gift of love is in her liberty:
  But, close thy door—then she is in her sky!

WITH SOME OLD LETTERS.

Old lips that speak no more I hear;
  Old vanish'd faces, brightening, come;
Old footsteps echo, strangely near,
  From happy doors of Home!—

I feel the quick blood of the Past
  Beat through Time's veins again in light;
I see warm hands, from loving hearts
  Extended, while they write!

A DECEMBER NIGHT.

Listen!—the wind is crying, like a loon
On some far water, and the rising moon
Stands breathless on the snow! That wind!—it seems
A lost soul crying out in holy dreams,
The cry of some long unappeased despair
That has no human tongue—a soul in the air!
The flame drops into ember-breathing gloom;
Glimmers of shadow walk around the room,
Great shapeless shapes, a shuddering moment plain,
As the flame drops, then vanishing again!

NEW FLIGHTS.

How glad yet sad is he whom gods have given,
With wings that lift him ever toward their Heaven,
The sight that looks beyond the farthest star
And sees, each higher flight, the Heaven more far!

FORMER SELF.

LIFE's task-work comes, after our youthful dreams,
And we forget in drudgeries of earth
Those bodily wings that took our dreams to Heaven,
Now heavy-drooping, soil'd, invisible,
Unlifted and unconscious by our sides.
Yet there are times when we remember them,
And vaguely feel their old and buoyant power
And dream its restoration suddenly,
But for a moment only—dropping down
We recognize the vanish'd angelhood,
Care-burden'd men whose footprints pass in dust.

SNOW-FALLING.

THE wonderful Snow is falling,
Over river and woodland and wold;
The trees bear spectral blossom
In the moonshine blurr'd and cold.

There's a beautiful garden in Heaven;
And these are the banish'd flowers,
Falling and driven and drifted
Into this dark world of ours!

HALF-DREAMING.

TO ——, IN ABSENCE.

THEY come, in long procession rise before
My wakeful sight, most gentle thoughts of thee
And of thy love, the dearest dream to me
That ever grew dear truth for evermore;
And as a child in his still bed—the door
Half-open where his mother's light may be
A comfort to his lonely sense when he,
Though waking, feels warm slumber reach the core
Of his fresh spirit—drops his lids at last
To visit Fairyland, and numberless
Lithe shadows pass and shapes created fast,
Charming him till he sleeps, and are his dream:
So, while I wake in home-sick dreaminess,
My thoughts of thee through dreamful visions gleam.

BEARERS OF THE WORLD.

I THOUGHT of that grave Fable of the Past,
World-shouldering Atlas, and I slept at noon.

Then wandering shadows, wavering out of dreams,
(From men once sweating in the sun,) I saw,
Stooping and groaning, pass—like those beheld
In Purgatory by the Florentine,
Bow'd down with penance. And these utter'd cries
Of sharp complaint continuous, wailing blind
At the deaf Providence that would not see
Nor lift their woful burdens. Each one cried:
"Most wretched Atlas, for I bear the world!"
And vanish'd in some barren space of sand.

Then others follow'd—burden'd like to those
That pass'd before lamenting—crown'd with peace,
Silent with dews of patience in their breasts,
Or with long sorrows hush'd on prayerful lips,
Or cheerful-brow'd, with forward-looking smiles
Of tender welcome for the wayside friends
By Nature sent to meet them—flower, and bird,
And tree, and fountain-head, and dancing brook;
And some with eyes uplifted came, like him
Who dropp'd his pack at the Celestial Gate,
White with the years and wayworn with the dust.
And each one, leaning onward ever, said:
"Most happy Atlas, for I bear the world!"—
Vanishing in the gateways of a Land
Green with the pastures of a Paradise.

AFTERWARD.

NO more? Through all the years to meet
  No more? No more! Alas, no more!
I pray thy lips may smile as sweet—
  Unblest, I bless thee as before;
In solitudes of men apart
  My life's blind flowers for their dawn
Shall grope and climb—into thy heart;
  And grow—in dreams of sunshine gone!

No more? Through all the years to meet
  No more? No more! Alas, no more!
The tide that in my heart has beat
  May ebb, but still must haunt the shore

And leave vague shells of thought to lie
  And murmur evermore of thee;
On barren sand, until I die,
  The tide-mark of my love shall be.

No more? Through all the years to meet
  No more? No more! Alas, no more!
Yet oft from embers, strange and sweet,
  Shall start the flame so sweet before.
Again thy face I may not see,
  But still thy spirit in mine shall rise;
The violets over graves shall be,
  And from their souls shall look thine eyes.

TRANSFIGURATION.

[CHARLESTOWN, VA., DEC. 2, 1859.
WASHINGTON, D. C., DEC. 2, 1863.*]

FOUR years ago the Savior of the Slave
Took in his strong, brave arms a slave-born child—
Ere from the gallows to the martyr's grave
He pass'd—with manly blessing, deep and mild.

O Land, however strong, too weak to do
Such office then! Like Christopher of old,

* It seemed a suggestive coincidence, that Crawford's Statue of Freedom (the work of putting which in bronze was said to have been executed by negroes who were, or had been, slaves in the employ of Clark Mills) was raised to its position on the dome of the National Capitol on the anniversary of the execution at Charlestown, four years previous, and at the same hour of the day.

In that poor child the lifted Christ he knew,
  The great bond-breaker in his human hold!

O humbled Nation! To thy proudest place
  Thou liftest yonder shape of Freedom now,
Where Morning shall be quick to see her face,
  And Eve to touch with dew her sacred brow!

But he who seeks the soul within the form
  In that bright shape shall see another sight:
A gray old man, holding, in calm or storm,
  The unfetter'd child forever in the light!

TWO WATCHERS.

TWO ships sail on the ocean;
  Two watchers walk the shore:
One wrings wild hands and cries,
  "Farewell for evermore."

One sees, with face uplifted,
  (Soft homes of dream her eyes,)
Her sail, beyond the horizon,
  Reflected in the skies!

A MAN'S VOTE.

[NOVEMBER, 1864.]

GO down into the ballot-box—from no unconscious hand—
And, rising on the morrow morn, ring out through all the Land!
Go down into the ballot-box, my single vote, to-night:
Ring with a myriad, single-voiced, abroad in morning light!

Go down into the ballot-box, a righteous vote and true—
No patriot's blood shall wasted seem, no bondman's dream, for you!

Go down into the ballot-box, unheard, unfelt, unknown:
You shall be heard and felt and seen—the Day for you'll be shown!

If all the morn I held you fast, in silence and apart,
It matters not, O vote, you know I kept you in my heart!
Go down into the ballot-box—for Right at any cost;
And, what though last?—the polls are closed—thank God, you are not lost!

PARTING AND MEETING.

O WINGS of parting, heavy!
  O wings of meeting, light!
We part—the shadows hover;
  We meet—the world is bright!

We part—the birds at sunset
  Fold round their songs their wings;
We meet—the sun arises,
  The lark in Heaven sings!

A ROSE'S JOURNEY.

HASTE on your gentle journey, sent
To sweetest goal flower ever went:
Ah me, that can not follow close—
But my heart runs before you, rose!

O happy rose, I envy you—
But sweetness makes such sweet grace due:
First to her lips one moment press'd—
Then your long Heaven on her dear breast!

ARMY OF THE POTOMAC.

[WASHINGTON, MAY, 1865.]

SOLDIERS, return'd from many a fight, to-day
I call another year, another May:
Then from your homes at first ye march'd away.

Your country summon'd—what quick answer came
Shall never be forgot by human fame:
The North was red with one electric flame!

The dragon's teeth were sown that started men—
(So may the Land be never sown again!)
Ye were the crop that sprang in armor then.

Lo, every highway made its end in one,
With stern advancing dust against the sun!—
A line of bayonets thrust to Washington!

I heard, I saw!—the street ye tread to-day
Took echoes that shall never pass away,
Visions that shall be visible for aye!

——Ye come from many a long-remember'd fight:
Your flags are glittering, in the windy light,
With names that make their tremulous stars more
bright.

Banners whose rags are famous, veterans too,
Pathetic with the storms they flutter'd through,
Ye bear in pride and tenderness with you!

Ye come—ye are not all that went away:
Another myriad, great as yours, to-day
Keep their encampment with the flowers of May.

——Ye came from homes that haply echo still
With your last footsteps on the quiet sill:
Go back, go back, the empty air to fill!

Ye came from new-plow'd fields and wheated lands,
Where the old harvests call'd for willing hands:
Go back to join the gentle reaper bands!

Ye came—the work is done ye came to do:
Go back, go back, O servants tried and true—
Go back to find your Land created new!

TWO RETURNS.

LAST night I found your gentle face
 Within the household air you bless;
 The gather'd rays of happiness
Touch'd all things in the hearth-warm'd place.

Last night I dream'd a weird, sad dream:
 The moonrise shiver'd through the trees,
 With a low-moaning autumn breeze,
And fleck'd the roof with ghostly gleam.

Through frost-furr'd rose-vines warmly cast,
 Welcoming arms of household flame
 Reach'd forth to meet me as I came
And clasp me in from all the Past.

Glad voices made the walls alive
  With murmur-music: loving sound
  That even the world's far echoes found—
Lost bees of Love in Memory's hive!

I paused, I listen'd: you were there!—
  A moment and the wander'd years
  Would melt in smiles or drown in tears,
And change would pass away in air!

I knock'd: your footsteps lightly came,
  And drew old music from my heart——
  Oh, opening door! I stood apart:
Darkness!—no voice, no face, no flame!

No hurrying warmth of happy air,
  Though the dear chimney rosily

Clasp'd close some lighted family:
You were not there, you were not there!

"The wind!" half-whisper'd some one. Then
The Summer shut the Winter out:
The startled child with eager shout
Climb'd mother-knees secure again!

The walls were glad with laugh and shout:
Returning young, and lithe and gay,
Who shiver'd there so old and gray?—
The Summer shut the Winter out.

And where were you? Dead years replied,
Slow, one by one.
——— Another tone,
The dream in blissful waking flown,
Gave back the happy-hearted tide!

Snow warm'd to flowers by April air,
  How brightly fell those dreadful years!
  Lo, all my heart lay fresh in tears—
Your morning voice was on the stair!

TO THE STATUE ON THE CAPITOL:

LOOKING EASTWARD AT DAWN.

WHAT sunken splendor in the Eastern skies
Seest thou, O Watcher, from thy lifted place?—
Thine old Atlantic dream is in thine eyes,
But the new Western morning on thy face.

Beholdest thou, in reäpparent light,
Thy lost Republics? They were visions, fled.
Their ghosts in ruin'd cities walk by night—
It is no resurrection of their dead.

But look, behind thee, where in sunshine lie
  Thy boundless fields of harvest in the West,
Whose savage garments from thy shoulders fly,
  Whose eagle clings in sunrise to thy crest!

WASHINGTON, D. C.

IN MARCH.

WELCOME, sweet Wind; you bring
        A soul of Spring
From some far, fragrant rose,
        That blows
In some dear, coming May, or half-forgotten Spring.

Welcome, sweet Dream; you bear
        Your wings of air
From some far isle of love—
        A dove,
Flying with gentle bough from some far, lovelier
        air.

What though the sweet Wind knows
A vanish'd rose—
My dream the Past, alone,
Has known ?—
Bloom from my heart, sweet dream ; climb from my dream, sweet rose !

THE BUBBLE-BLOWERS.

JOYOUS faces in the sunshine,
Happy laughter, tossing hair!
See the children blowing bubbles,
Worlds in bright-enchanted air!

Worlds, their merry new creations—
Fairy globes for lifted eyes!
In the sunshine rise the bubbles—
From their hearts the fairies rise!

WITH SOME SHELLS AND POEMS.

TAKE up these little sea-shells, Dear,
And press them closely to your ear:
Their vague and desolate monotone
Saddens you with its ceaseless moan,
As if the ocean, prison'd there,
Moved with a vast but dumb despair.

Deep in those cells of subtle sound
Some boundless spirit seems prison-bound,
Murmuring of shores where wrecks are strown
And ghosts of tempests walk alone,
Yet, over all—from all apart—
You hear the beatings of your heart.

Take now these poems, vague with woe,
Found with the sea-shells long ago:
Within you hear the sounds that swell
From restless seas and haunt the shell;
But listen, and your heart shall let
New music silence old regret.

www.ingramcontent.com/pod-product-compliance
Lightning Source LLC
LaVergne TN
LVHW021427110826
845150LV00007B/2117

* 9 7 8 1 4 2 5 5 0 7 4 1 1 *